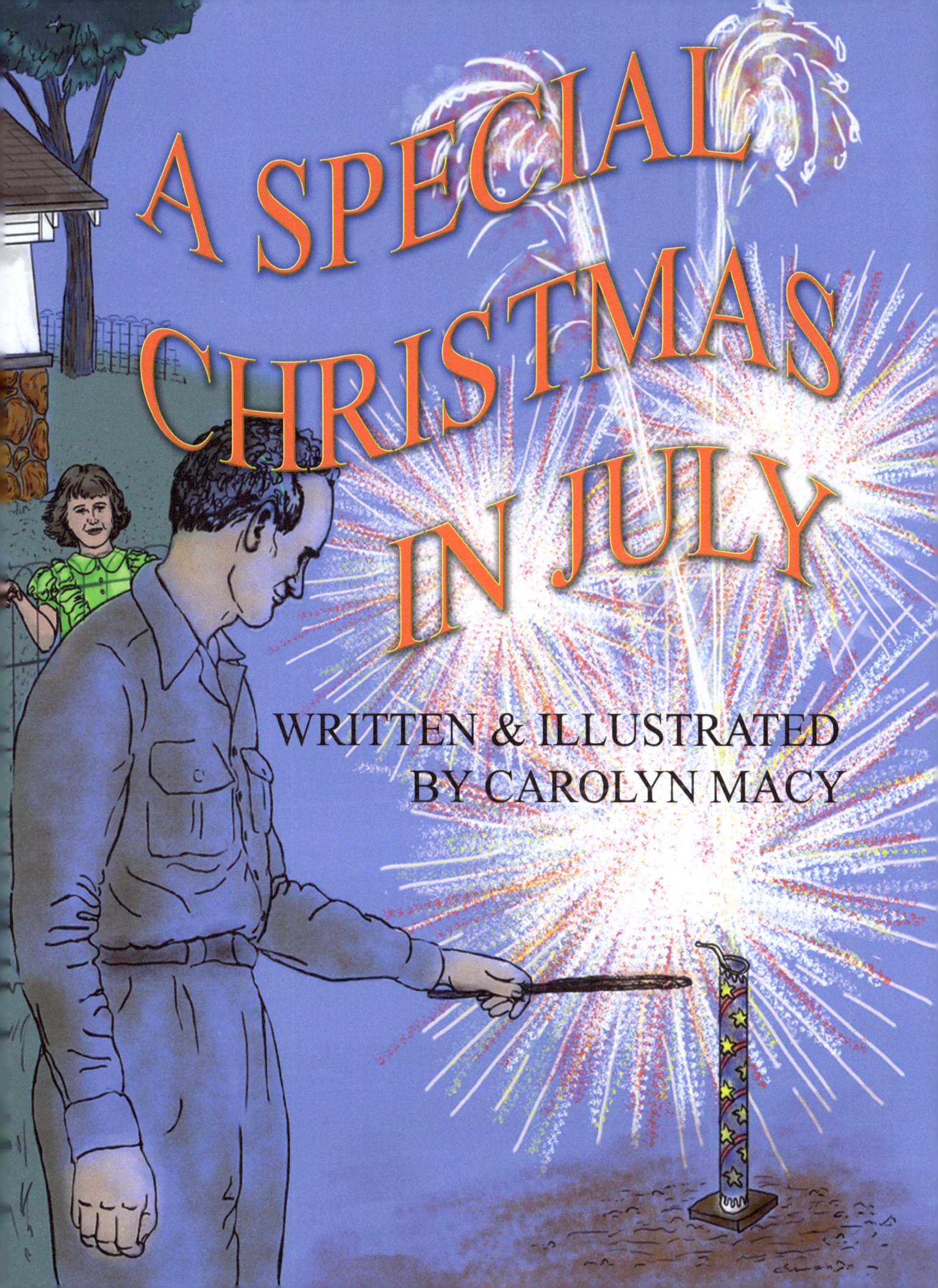

Dedicated to my family and friends, particularly to my sisters, Margaret and Francie, and my cousin, David, for their help in memories and pictures.

A Special Christmas in July
Copyright © 2017 by Carolyn Macy. All rights reserved.

No part of this publication may be reproduced, stored in a retrieval system or transmitted in any way by any means, electronic, mechanical, photocopy, recording or otherwise without the prior permission of the author except as provided by USA copyright law.

Published by Carolyn Macy
6227 81st Avenue N.E. | Norman, Oklahoma 73026 USA
405.401.2012

Book design copyright © 2017 by Carolyn Macy.
Written and Illustrated by Carolyn Macy

Published in the United States of America
ISBN: 978-0-9988838-0-9
JUVENILE NONFICTION / Biography & Autobiography

Part 1: The Letter...

Today a letter came
 From Uncle Clyde which read,
 "Next week we'll bring the boys
 To spend the month ahead."

We counted down the days
  When cousins would appear
To stay at Grandma's house
  And visit us this year!

Within our grove of trees,
We built a place to play,
But found it leaked a lot
One very rainy day.

When moonlight filled the sky
And stars above popped out,
We watched the wonders there
With night sounds all about.

By living where we did,

We sometimes had to face

Our stopping play to help
With work around the place.

Each day became so full,

For we found much to do.
So as we worked and played,
The summer quickly flew.

Part 3: Why Christmas came in July...

But then one day a sound
That came from overhead
Caused all of us to stop
And look above instead.

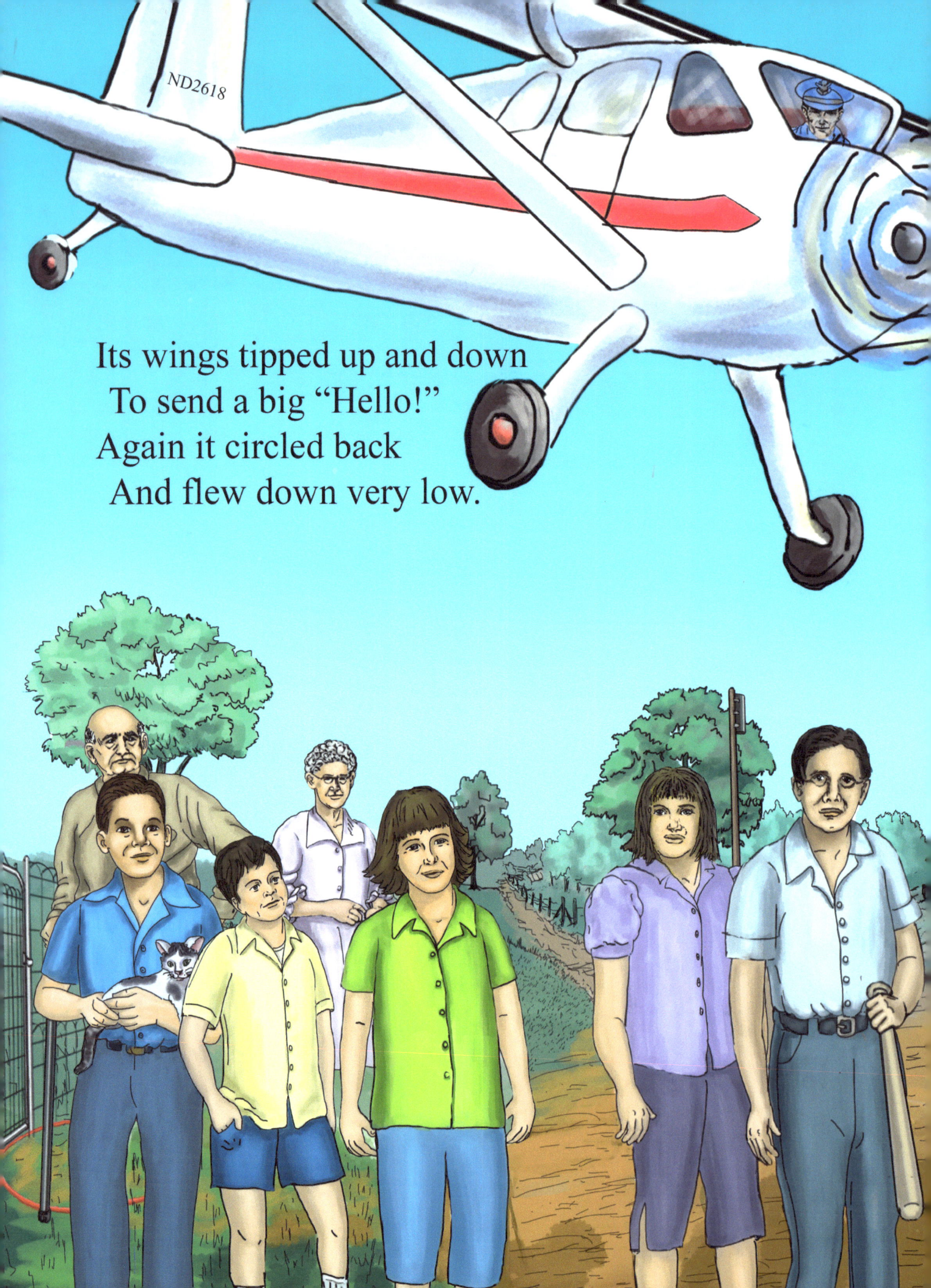

Its wings tipped up and down
 To send a big "Hello!"
Again it circled back
 And flew down very low.

As we kept watching him,
His plane dipped low again

So he could drop a bag
 Of treasures packed within.

We opened up the bag
Delivered through the air,

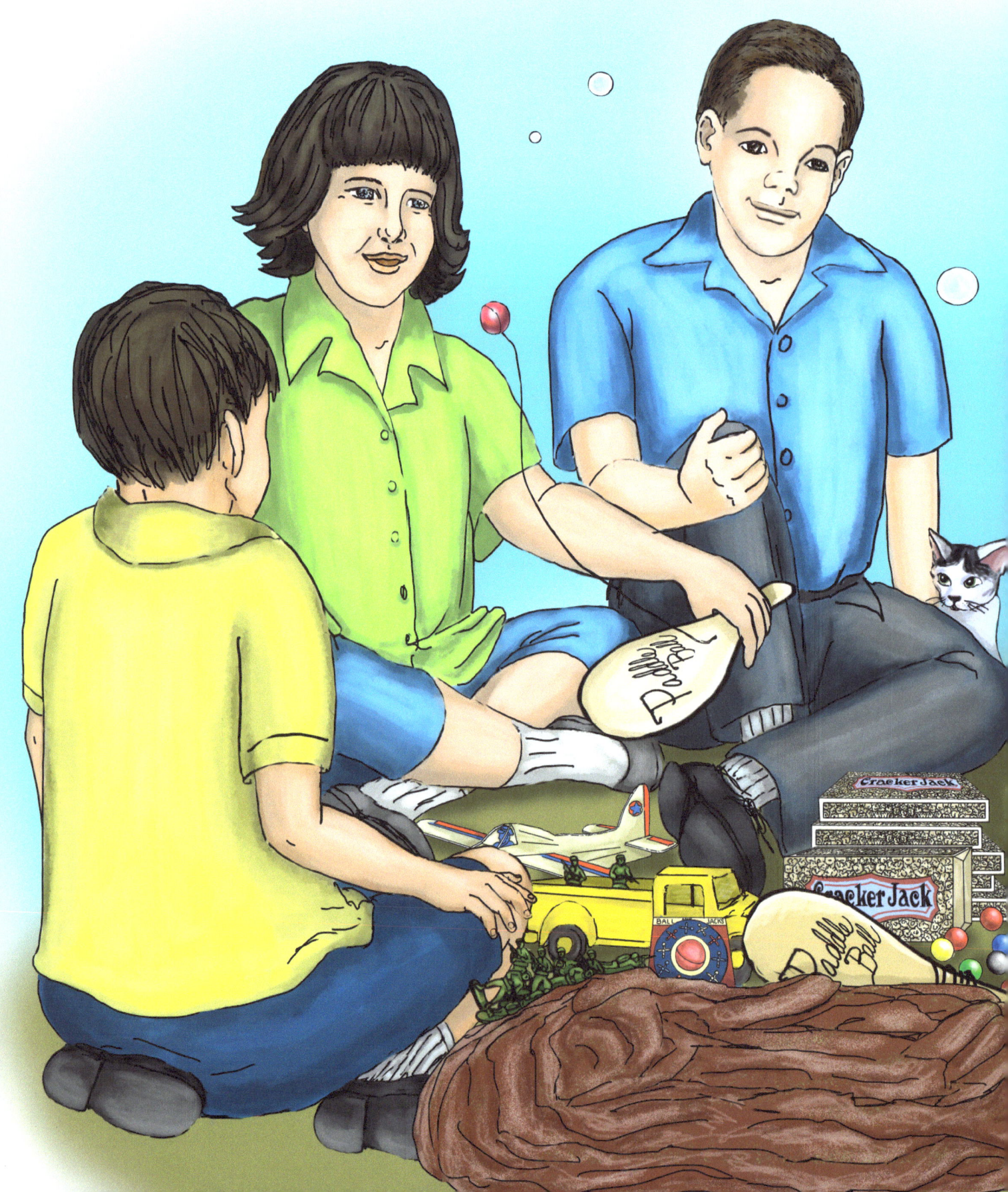

To see what treats it held
For all of us to share.

Delighted with his gifts,
We made a quick reply
To thank our Uncle Clyde
For 'Christmas in July'!